D0100024

Kids in the Kitchen

Kids in the Kitchen

100 Delicious, Fun & Healthy
Recipes to Cook & Bake

Micah Pulleyn &
Sarah Bracken

A Sterling/Lark Book
Sterling Publishing Co., Inc.   New York

Editor: Carol Taylor
Art Director: Kathleen Holmes
Photography: Evan Bracken
Production: Elaine Thompson and Kathleen Holmes

Library of Congress Cataloging-in-Publication Data
Pulleyn, Micah
      Kids in the kitchen : 100 delicious, fun, and healthy recipes to cook
and bake / Micah Pulleyn and Sarah Bracken.
         p.   cm.
      "A Sterling/Lark book."
      Includes index.
      ISBN 0-8069-0447-X
      1. Cookery–Juvenile literature.   [1. cookery.]   I. Bracken, Sarah.
II. Title.
TX652.5.P85   1994
641.5'123–dc20

93-39111
CIP
AC

10 9 8 7 6 5 4 3 2 1

A Sterling/Lark Book

Published in 1994 by Sterling Publishing Co., Inc.
   387 Park Ave. S., New York, NY 10016

Created and produced by Altamont Press, Inc.
   50 College St., Asheville, NC 28801

© 1994, Altamont Press

Distributed in Canada by Sterling Publishing,
   c/o Canadian Manda Group, P.O. Box 920, Station U, Toronto,
   Ontario M8Z 5P9
Distributed in the United Kingdom by Cassell PLC, Villiers House,
   41/47 Strand, London WC2N 5JE, England
Distributed in Australia by Capricorn Link (Australia) Pty Ltd.
   P.O. Box 6651, Baulkham Hills, Business Centre, NSW 2153, Australia

Every effort has been made to ensure that all information in this book is
accurate. However, due to differing conditions, tools, and individual skills,
the publisher cannot be responsible for any injuries, losses, or other
damages which may result from the use of the information in this book.

All rights reserved.

Printed in Hong Kong

ISBN 0-8069-0447-X

Contents

Introduction

Welcome to *Kids in the Kitchen!* We're glad you decided to join us in one of the nicest rooms in the house. We like to cook, and we think learning to cook is a great thing for a kid to do.

Why?

It's fun.

You know those rainy afternoons when you're bored and you don't know what to do with yourself? There's nothing on TV and you don't have a book you want to read right now and, besides, you're too restless to sit still…

Go to the kitchen and cook something! If you have another hobby—like building model airplanes or collecting dolls—you know how much fun it is to get completely absorbed in doing something, how the time seems to fly past.

It's the same with cooking. Once you concentrate on making something good to eat, you're not bored or restless anymore.

You can have things the way you want them.

Of course, it's nice to have somebody else cook for you. But other people usually cook things the way *they* like. (Makes sense, right?) If you cook for yourself, you can go ahead and put the peanut butter on the celery, no matter what anybody else thinks about it.

It feels good to be able to take care of yourself.

OK, what if you're by yourself or all the adults are busy and you're really hungry? If you know how to cook, no problem! You don't have to wait for somebody to come home or to finish what they're doing. You can just go ahead and make yourself something good to eat.

Of course, when you're home alone, stick to recipes that don't require sharp knives or hot stoves. There are lots of great dishes in this book that don't need either one!

You get good things to eat.

If you're like most people, you like to eat! That's maybe the best thing about this hobby. When you're finished, you've got something great to snack on.

It's fun to cook with other people, too.

If you have a friend over, the two of you can have a good time cooking together. You can cook with a parent…with a brother or sister…even with a babysitter.

Everybody can learn to cook!

Cooking isn't hard, but it does take some learning and some practice. So, of course, you'll probably make a few mistakes. (We certainly do!)

Don't get discouraged! You'll probably learn something from every one of those "failures." For one thing, you'll learn what doesn't work, and that's always good to know. The more you cook, the better you'll get. And the better you'll eat! And the more fun you'll have.

So get out the measuring spoons and the mixer and whatever else you need. And join in the fun!

Here are a few of the things we've learned—sometimes the hard way—that make cooking easier, safer, and more fun.

Get Ready, Get Set . . .

▼ Before you begin to cook, check the number of servings the recipe will make. Will there be enough?

▼ Read the recipe all the way through before you start cooking.

▼ Collect everything you need to prepare the recipe, including equipment and ingredients.

▼ Make sure you have enough of each ingredient.

▼ Always set a timer when the recipe says to cook for a certain number of minutes.

Safety

▼ Be very careful with knives. If you feel uncomfortable cutting something, ask a grown-up to help.

▼ Use pot holders when handling anything hot or warm. Be extra careful with boiling water.

▼ Turn all pot handles away from kitchen traffic so that nobody bumps into a hot pot and knocks it over.

▼ When removing a lid from a hot pan or baking dish, raise the back of the lid first, so the hot steam escapes away from you. Then lift the lid all the way off and stand back out of the way while the rest of the steam leaves the pan.

▼ Always turn the oven and/or stove-top dials to "off" as soon as you finish with them.

▼ Ask a grown-up for help if you need it. We can't always do everything by ourselves, and kitchen help always makes cooking much more fun.

▼ If you have long hair, pull it back out of the way. If you have long sleeves, roll them up.

Inside Information

▼ When cutting something, always use a cutting board so your kitchen counter tops don't get scratched.

▼ If a recipe calls for butter or margarine, take it out of the refrigerator half an hour before you need it, so it isn't too hard to work with.

RULES AND TIPS

▼ When measuring butter in a measuring cup, wet the cup before putting the butter in, so it will slide right out.

▼ When using a raw egg, crack it into a small bowl or cup, and make sure there are no little pieces of eggshell in it. Then add it to your mixture. That way, you won't get any shells in your food.

▼ When you're gathering ingredients for a recipe, don't set the eggs right on the counter top—they could roll off and splatt onto the floor. Put them in a little bowl.

▼ Store leftover food for snacking later, and keep unused ingredients for future use.

▼ Ask a friend to come over and make something with you. Some of the best food is made by a cooperating team.

▼ Add, change, and experiment with these recipes. Our tastes will not always be like yours, so try to make the food the way you like it.

▼ Write in this book. If you change a recipe and it turns out well, you'll probably want to do the same thing again. Make a note to yourself so you can remember what you did.

▼ Share this book with your friends. Let other people in on your cooking secrets, and give them the chance to have fun in the kitchen. You might even bring it to class with you and make a snack, or even lunch, for everyone.

Clean-up Hints

▼ Always wash your hands with soap and water before you begin, even if you won't be directly touching the food. It's hard to cook with nasty, gross, disgusting hands.

▼ When making messy foods, wear an apron and old clothes.

▼ Leave the kitchen extra clean when you are done. Put everything back in the right place and check to see that the stove is off. You will always be welcome to use the kitchen again if you leave it clean.

▼ Use cloth towels instead of paper towels to wipe up spills. This saves our beautiful trees.

▼ Put ingredients away as you use them.

▼ If you clean up as you go, you won't be stuck with all the boring work at the end.

TERMS

Cutting Terms

Chop: To cut into small pieces.

Coins: Pieces of food that are cut to look like money—for example, slices of banana.

Core: To cut out the stem and the seedy center of a fruit or vegetable, using a corer or a knife.

Cube: To cut into roughly square chunks about the size of your nose.

Cut In: A way of adding butter, margarine, or shortening to dry ingredients without blending them completely. Place the butter in the dry ingredients and use a pastry cutter to cut the chunks of butter into very fine "gravel."

Dice: To chop into *very* small pieces.

Grate: To shred by rubbing against a grater. Usually you'll grate cheese or carrots.

Peel: To remove the outer skin of a fruit or vegetable, using a peeler or a knife.

Mixing Terms

Beat: To stir something quickly and hard with a whisk or electric mixer, to mix it up and make it fluffy.

Blend: To mix completely by stirring or by spinning it in a blender, till you can't find the separate ingredients anymore and you have a whole new mixture.

Dissolve: To stir a dry ingredient into liquid until the dry part seems to disappear.

Fold: To mix ingredients by slowly and gently turning one over another, using a rubber spatula. Usually, egg whites are folded into a batter so they don't lose their fluffiness.

Knead: To use your hands to push, turn, press, and fold dough so that all the air bubbles get pushed out.

Toss: To gently mix the ingredients of a salad by lifting them up with your hands or with two spoons and dropping them back in the bowl.

Whip: To beat ingredients at very high speed until the mixture is light and fluffy, using a whisk or an electric mixer.

Cooking Terms

Bake: To cook in the oven with the heat coming from below the food. It takes a while to heat and cook the food fully.

Boil: To heat liquid in a pan on the stove until bubbles break the surface.

Broil: To cook in the oven with all the heat coming from *above* the food. This browns the food quickly and may burn it, so watch it carefully.

Brown: To broil, fry, or bake food until it turns golden brown.

Melt: To make a solid into a liquid by placing it over low heat.

Overcook: To leave food in the oven or on the stove too long. If this happens, it usually turns tough, burns, or begins to burn.

Preheat: To turn the oven on before you start a recipe or before you put something in the oven. This lets the oven get to the right temperature by the time you're ready to bake the food.

Simmer: To leave on low heat so that the food is very hot but not boiling. Bubbles will form slowly but won't rise all the way to the surface.

Steam: To cook food over boiling water in the hot, rising steam. Place the food on a rack, then put the rack in a large pot. Put water in the bottom of the pot, and cover it with the lid. Heat the water until it boils and makes steam, which cooks the food. Steaming is especially good for fresh vegetables.

Other Terms

Air-dry: To allow something to dry naturally by letting it sit out in the air.

Drain: To pour liquid off a solid. One way is to pour everything—solid and liquid—into a strainer or colander and let the liquid run out the bottom.

Drizzle: To pour just a little liquid slowly, in a thin stream, on top of something.

Grease: To add a thin coating of butter, vegetable oil, or margarine on a baking sheet, muffin pan, or other cooking utensil to keep the food from sticking to it.

Grease and Flour: To sprinkle flour on a greased baking pan, to keep the food from sticking to it.

Liquefy: To spin food in the blender or food processor until it turns into a thick liquid.

Marinate: To soak food in a liquid that will add flavor and, in some cases, make the food tender.

Roll: To flatten and spread dough with a rolling pin, to make it even and thin.

Separate Eggs: To separate the white from the yolk. To do this, place a clean bowl on the counter top or table, and crack the eggshell across the middle by hitting the egg against the counter. Holding the egg over the bowl, carefully open the shell and let the white fall into the bowl. Pour the yolk back and forth between the two halves of the shell until all the white is in the bowl. Then put the yolk in another bowl.

MEASURING NOTES

Careful measuring is really important when you're cooking, especially
when you're making a new recipe.
Later, you'll know what you can add
more of if you want to (raisins in
your cookies, for example) and what
you can't change without hurting the
recipe (such as baking powder).

Tips

▼ When measuring a dry ingredient—like
flour or white sugar—fill the measuring cup or
spoon so it's heaped up over the top. Then
hold the cup over a bowl and level it off by
scraping across the top with the flat edge of a
knife. This makes your measuring exact.

▼ Brown sugar is measured in a different
way from white sugar. It must be pressed
tightly into whatever container you're measuring with. You can use the back of a spoon or
your clean hands to pack the brown sugar
into the measuring cup or spoon.

▼ If you are doubling a recipe, or halving it,
always ask a grown-up for help to make sure
the measurements are correct.

Temperature

Fahrenheit	Celsius
300	150
325	165
350	175
375	190
400	205

Actually, you will come close enough if you
just divide degrees Fahrenheit by 2 to get
degrees Celsius.

Metric Measurements

If you're using the metric system of weights and measures, here's how to convert the amounts in the recipes.

Liquid Measurements (volume)
1 cup = 240 ml = 1/4 liter
3/4 cup = 180 milliliters
2/3 cup = 160 milliliters
1/2 cup = 120 milliliters
1/3 cup = 80 milliliters
1/4 cup = 60 milliliters
1 quart = 1 liter

Dry Measurements (weight)
1 ounce = 30 grams
2 ounces = 60 grams
8 ounces = 1/2 pound = 230 grams
1 pound = 460 grams

What equals what?

A table like this can come in handy when you have questions about measurements.

3 teaspoons = 1 tablespoon
1-1/2 teaspoons = 1/2 tablespoon
4 tablespoons = 1/4 cup
8 tablespoons = 1/2 cup
16 tablespoons = 1 cup
1 cup = 1/2 pint
2 cups = 1 pint
4 cups = 1 quart
2 pints = 1 quart
1 cup = 8 fluid ounces
32 ounces = 1 quart
2 quarts = 1/2 gallon
4 quarts = 1 gallon
1 stick of butter = 8 tablespoons = 1/2 cup

Measuring Notes 13

The Big Banana Wrap-Up

1 Serving

You can make banana-baked-in-bread just for yourself or for a whole crowd. This is a sweet and warm breakfast treat that tastes great with low-fat yogurt. It's truly a delicious breakfast!

What You'll Need

1 slice bread

1 teaspoon honey

1/2 tablespoon jelly or preserves

1/2 banana

1/2 tablespoon butter

1/2 teaspoon cinnamon

What to do

1. Preheat the oven or toaster oven to 400°F.

2. Roll the bread flat with a rolling pin, and trim off the crusts. Then spread the honey and jelly on the bread with a butter knife.

3. Place the banana half on the bread, and roll them up.

4. Melt the butter in a small saucepan over low heat.

5. Roll the bread-covered banana in melted butter, and bake it in a baking dish for 15 minutes, until the bread is crisp and the banana is hot and creamy.

6. When it's done, sprinkle the bread-covered banana with cinnamon—and presto! Breakfast!

Oatmeal Pancakes

Makes 10 to 12 4-inch Pancakes

Even if you pretty much live on breakfast cereals already, this may be the best way to eat oatmeal that anybody ever thought of. Try it; it's incredibly dee-lish!

What You'll Need

1-1/4 cups milk

1 cup rolled oats

2 eggs

1 tablespoon vegetable oil

1/2 cup whole wheat flour

3 tablespoons granulated sugar

1 teaspoon baking powder

1/4 teaspoon salt

1/4 teaspoon cinnamon

What to do

1. Combine the milk and rolled oats in a large mixing bowl. Allow the oats to soak for at least five minutes (this softens them up).

2. Beat the eggs in a small bowl with a whisk.

3. Add the eggs and the oil to the oats, and mix well. Stir in the flour, sugar, baking powder, salt, and cinnamon.

4. Cook on a hot, lightly oiled griddle or frying pan, using about 1/4 cup of batter for each pancake. Turn them when the edges are slightly brown. Make sure they get cooked all the way through to the middle.

Banana Fiesta

If you enjoy new ways to eat bananas, here's your perfect recipe. This will warm up your tummy and make your taste buds happy! Breakfast doesn't always have to be cold cereal and toast, so check this out!

What You'll Need

3 bananas

1 tablespoon butter

6 eggs

1/2 cup raisins

1 teaspoon cinnamon

1-1/2 cups yogurt (if you wish)

What to do

1. Peel the bananas and cut them into thick coins. In a frying pan, saute the bananas in the butter until they're browned.

2. Beat the eggs with a whisk in a small bowl, then add raisins and cinnamon.

3. Cook the egg mixture in a saucepan on low heat.

4. Add the bananas to the egg mixture, and serve.

5. It tastes even better if you put yogurt on top!

All Scrambled Up

Spicy, fixed-up eggs are a terrific change from regular scrambled eggs. People who live in the Southwest, near the Mexican border, really know how to make eggs taste great. Sabrosa!

What You'll Need

4 medium eggs

1/2 cup salsa (see recipe on page 101, if you need one)

1/2 cup sour cream

1 cup grated cheese

What to do

1. Scramble the eggs in a frying pan over medium heat. When they're ready, divide them evenly between two plates.

2. Top the eggs with the salsa, sour cream, and cheese.

Jungle Yogurts

These jungle yogurt mixes are a great way to wake up each morning. The best thing about them is you can add or change anything you want. If you want two at one time, go for it! Just mix the recipes. If you find a wacky new idea, write it down.

What You'll Need

Very Berry:

    1-1/2 cups plain yogurt

    1/2 cup fresh strawberries, halved

    1/4 cup fresh blueberries

    1/4 teaspoon vanilla extract

Banana-Peach:

    1-1/2 cups plain yogurt

    3/4 cup fresh peach chunks

    1 teaspoon lemon juice

    1/2 banana cut into thin coins

    1/4 teaspoon vanilla extract

Apple Cinnamon:

    1-1/2 cups plain yogurt

    3/4 cup grated apple

    1/4 cup raisins or chopped almonds

    1/4 teaspoon vanilla extract

    1/4 teaspoon cinnamon

GORPola:

- 1-1/2 cups plain yogurt
- 1/2 cup granola (use recipe on page 28, if needed)
- 1/4 cup GORP (use recipe on page 35, if needed)
- 1 teaspoon honey

What to do

1. Gently combine all the ingredients of the recipe.

2. Serve chilled.

French Toast Sandwich

This is an even better version of old-fashioned French toast. We have added some sweet ingredients that we like, but feel free to add some of your own. The best recipes need your imagination to make them turn out the way you want.

What You'll Need

1 teaspoon honey

1 tablespoon peanut butter

1 egg

1/4 teaspoon cinnamon

2 tablespoons milk

2 slices of bread

2 slices of cheese

What to do

1. In a small bowl, stir together the honey and the peanut butter.

2. Whip the egg in a small bowl, using a whisk. Add the milk and cinnamon to the egg.

3. Spread the honey-peanut butter on one slice of bread.

4. Place the cheese slices on the honey-peanut butter. Put the other slice of bread on top of the cheese, to make a sandwich.

5. Dip the sandwich in the egg mixture, and saute it in a lightly buttered pan over medium heat. Cut it into smaller pieces and eat!

French Toast

French people call their special way of toasting bread "Lost Bread," because it uses stale bread that would otherwise be thrown away, or lost. If you make French Toast with bread that is too fresh, it will absorb too much of the egg and milk mixture and be soggy. YUCK!

Cheesy Apple Pancakes

Serve these pancakes to the family some chilly winter Saturday morning, to wake everyone up and get them started off just right. The whole family will love them—guaranteed. The pancakes do take some time, so you might want to team up with a brother, sister, or friend to make them.

What You'll Need

4 eggs

1 cup cottage cheese

1/4 cup grated apple

1/4 cup whole wheat flour

1 tablespoon honey

1/2 cup chopped almonds or cashews

1/2 teaspoon cinnamon

1/4 teaspoon allspice

1/2 teaspoon salt

What to do

1. Separate the eggs into two small bowls.

2. In a large mixing bowl, combine everything except the egg whites.

3. Beat the egg whites with an electric mixer until they are stiff, then fold them into the batter with a rubber spatula.

4. Cook on a hot, lightly oiled griddle or frying pan, using about 1/4 cup of batter for each pancake. Turn them when the edges are slightly brown. Make sure they get cooked all the way through to the middle.

5. Top with maple syrup, fresh fruit, jam or preserves, cottage cheese, and/or yogurt. Feel free to mix and match toppings.

2 Servings

Glorious Grapefruit

Some people believe that this fruit came from Jamaica, an island in the Caribbean Sea, south of the U.S. The grapefruit is a popular fruit nowadays, especially in Europe. The Dutch word for grapefruit is *pompelmoes*, which means "pumpkin lemon." The Spanish call it *toronja*—combining *toro*, which means "bull," and *naranja*, which means "orange."

Grapefruit Delight

Whenever we see a juicy grapefruit, we cut it open and add a sweet treat to it. Try this if you like grapefruit and you're looking for a new way to eat it.

What You'll Need

1 grapefruit

2 tablespoons brown sugar

What to do

1. Cut the grapefruit in half crosswise (between the two black spots).

2. Spoon the brown sugar on the cut parts, 1 tablespoon for each half. Eat with a spoon.

Simple Toasts

1 Serving

If you want something easy and fast, here's your answer to a morning snack. These are just a couple of ideas; if you find a good simple toast, write it down.

What You'll Need

Peanut Butter:

- 2 slices of your favorite bread
- 2 tablespoons peanut butter

Cream Cheese:

- 2 slices of raisin bread
- 2 tablespoons cream cheese

What to do

1. Toast the bread.

2. Spread the peanut butter or cream cheese on the bread. It's that easy!

Egg in a Hole

This is a traditional breakfast that your grandparents probably made. It is very easy, and it takes almost no time at all. If you have friends over to spend the night, make some for them. If you are super hungry, make more than one for yourself.

1 Serving

What You'll Need

1 slice of bread

1 egg

What to do

1. Make a hole in the center of the bread, using an upside-down glass. Place the bread in a lightly greased frying pan.

2. Crack the egg into the hole and allow it to cook. It's that easy!

An Egg of a Different Color

Chicken eggs are either brown or white, depending on the breed of hen that lays them. Rumor has it that brown chickens lay brown eggs and white chickens lay white eggs, but that's not really true. (What would a striped chicken lay?) The color of the shell has no effect on any other part of the egg; inside, they're just alike.

Granola and Milk

It seems that every kid who goes to summer camp loves granola. And after a long day, even the staff members go up to the kitchen after the campers' bedtime and snack on a bowl of granola and milk.

What You'll Need

1-1/2 cups granola (see recipe on page 28, if you need one)

1 cup low-fat milk

What to do

1. Put the granola and milk in a cereal bowl, and eat with a spoon. If you add cut-up fruit on the top, you'll have even more flavor and sweetness.

Morning Cake

This sweet treat is perfect for those Saturday mornings when even your neighbors can hear your stomach growling. If you like gingerbread, you'll love this spicy cake.

What You'll Need

1/3 cup melted butter or margarine

1 cup molasses

1 egg

1 cup orange juice

2-1/2 cups whole wheat flour

1 teaspoon baking soda

1 teaspoon cinnamon

2 teaspoons powdered ginger

1/2 teaspoon salt

1/2 cup raisins

What to do

1. Grease a 9-inch by 9-inch baking pan. Preheat the oven to 350°F.

2. In a large bowl, mix the butter and the molasses with an electric mixer. Beat in the egg and then the orange juice with the electric mixer.

3. In a medium bowl, stir together the flour, soda, cinnamon, ginger, and salt. Add the dry ingredients to the wet ingredients, then add the raisins. Stir everything together.

4. Pour the batter into the pan and bake for 40 minutes. To be sure the cake is done, stick a toothpick into the center of the cake. If the toothpick comes out dry, the cake is done. If there is wet batter on the toothpick, bake the cake for another 5 minutes and check again.

Good Morning! 27

Trail Mixes and More!

Grand Granola

Makes 4 quarts

Granola is one of the best inventions anyone ever thought up. Hurrah granola!

What You'll Need

1-1/2 cups almonds

10 cups rolled oats

1 cup sunflower seeds

1 cup cashews

1 cup wheat germ

1 cup dried apple pieces

1/2 cup vegetable oil

1/2 cup honey

6 ounces (or 3/4 cup) orange juice concentrate

What to do

1. Preheat the oven to 300°F.

2. Chop the almonds into smaller pieces. Mix all the dry ingredients in a large mixing bowl.

3. In a small saucepan, combine the oil, honey, and orange juice concentrate. Heat over low heat and stir until the mixture is pretty warm.

4. Pour the wet mixture into the dry ingredients, and mix well. You should use your clean hands for this to get each parti-cle covered with liquid. This is the secret to crunchy granola.

5. Spread the mixture in two large baking pans, and toast it in the oven for 1 hour and 15 minutes. Remove the pans from the oven and stir the granola well every 10 minutes. Granola is ready when golden brown but not dry. When done, turn the oven off and leave the granola in the oven overnight so that it will crisp up.

6. Make sure that the granola is cool before you put it in an airtight container. If it is not cool when you store it, it will get soggy.

That's a Lot of Granola

The average person eats a ton of food each year.

Pita Chips

These tasty, crunchy pieces of pita make great snack foods. Take a handful with you in the car, or eat some with your lunch. The secret to keeping them crunchy is storing them in an airtight container.

What You'll Need

2 large pitas

2 teaspoons vegetable oil

2 tablespoons parmesan cheese

1 teaspoon salt

2 teaspoons garlic powder

1 teaspoon oregano

What to do

1. Cut the pitas by separating the two halves and slicing the bread into triangles. Grease a baking sheet and place the pita pieces on the sheet. Brush the oil on the triangles.

2. Sprinkle the seasonings on the pita, and broil them for about 5 minutes. Make sure you don't burn the chips. Let them cool on the sheet, then store them in an airtight bag.

The Ultimate Trail Mixes

Trail mixes may be the best snacks ever. Put some in a bag to take with you on a hike, or pour a little in a bowl for an after-school snack. Any way you eat them, you'll love them!

What You'll Need

Tropical Dreams:

- 1 cup raisins
- 2 cups dried apricots, sliced
- 1-1/2 cups dried pineapple chunks
- 1-1/2 cups dried papaya
- 1 cup shredded coconut
- 2 cups banana chips
- 2 cups brazil nuts
- 1 cup chopped pecans
- 1 cup peanuts
- 2 teaspoons salt

Any Day Delight:

- 2 cups raisins
- 2 cups pumpkin seeds
- 1 cup almonds
- 1 cup sunflower seeds
- 1/2 cup peanuts
- 1/2 cup pecans
- 1/2 cup shredded coconut
- 1 teaspoon salt

Check This Out:

- 2 cups peanuts
- 3 cups mini pretzels
- 1 cup Wheat Chex cereal
- 1 cup Corn Chex cereal
- 1 cup almonds
- 2 cups ale nuts
- 2 cups sesame sticks
- 1 teaspoon garlic powder
- 1 teaspoon peanut oil

Oriental Mix:

- 2 cups peanuts
- 2 cups dried corn kernels
- 1 cup almonds
- 1 cup dried peas
- 3 cups rice snacks
- 1/2 cup sesame seeds
- 2 cups cashews
- 1 cup sunflower seeds
- 2 teaspoons salt

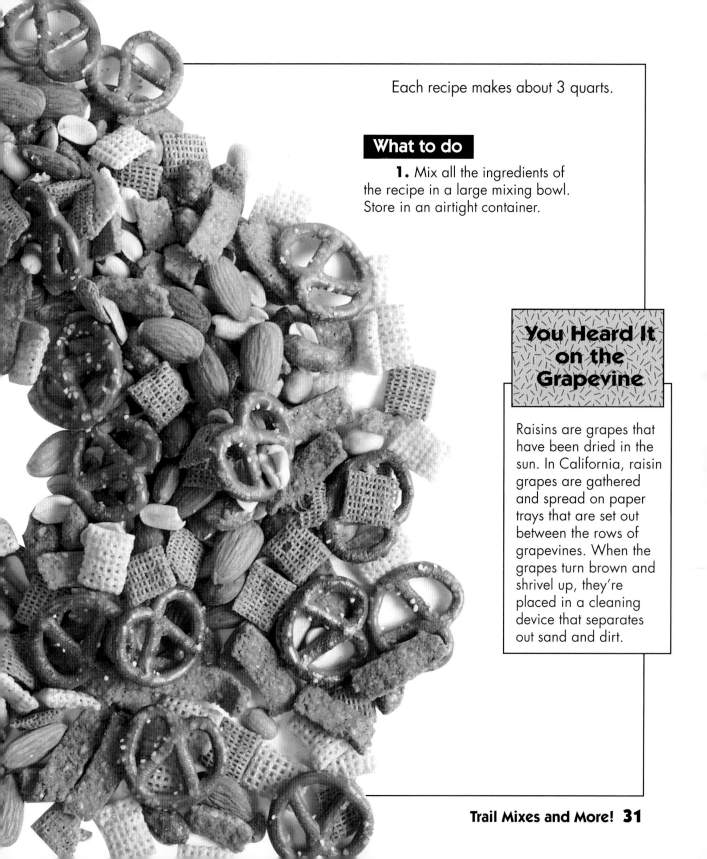

Each recipe makes about 3 quarts.

What to do

1. Mix all the ingredients of the recipe in a large mixing bowl. Store in an airtight container.

You Heard It on the Grapevine

Raisins are grapes that have been dried in the sun. In California, raisin grapes are gathered and spread on paper trays that are set out between the rows of grapevines. When the grapes turn brown and shrivel up, they're placed in a cleaning device that separates out sand and dirt.

Cornbread

Cornbread can be dry and plain, but it doesn't have to be! To make the sweetest, tenderest cornbread ever, keep an eye on it so that it doesn't burn, which is very hard to do! Top off a piece with apple butter or honey butter—either is yummy.

What You'll Need

1-1/4 cups yellow cornmeal (preferably unrefined)

1-1/4 cups whole wheat flour

2 teaspoons baking powder

1/3 teaspoon salt

1-1/4 cups milk

2 eggs

1/3 cup oil

1-1/2 cups honey

What to do

1. Preheat the oven to 350°F.

2. Grease a 10-inch by 14-inch baking pan.

3. Mix the dry ingredients together in a large mixing bowl.

4. Mix the wet ingredients in a smaller bowl, then pour the wet mixture into the dry ingredients.

5. Stir gently; don't get rid of all the lumps.

6. Bake for 30 to 35 minutes, until golden brown and firm to the touch.

Oatmeal Crackers

Makes 2 dozen

Here's a quick and easy idea for some great crackers. After you make them, try putting peanut butter, cheese, vegetables, or cream cheese on them. You can top them with wheat germ right before you put them in the oven, to make them more interesting.

What You'll Need

3/4 cup rolled oats

1/2 cup whole wheat flour

1/4 cup vegetable oil

1/2 tablespoon honey

1/4 cup water

1/4 cup sesame seeds

What to do

1. Preheat the oven to 350°F.

2. Put the oats in a blender and spin them until they are ground to a coarse flour.

3. Lightly grease a baking sheet.

4. Combine the oats and flour in a medium-sized bowl.

5. In a large bowl, mix the oil and honey together. Add the flour mixture and water, and stir just until dough is mixed well.

6. Roll the dough to a 1/8-inch thickness on the prepared baking sheet. Cut the dough into 2-inch squares with a sharp knife. Sprinkle the sesame seeds on the dough.

7. Bake for 12 to 15 minutes, or until golden brown, then cool for 10 minutes and remove the crackers from the baking sheet. Store in an airtight bag.

Animal Crackers

If you like animals and you like sweet crackers, you can put the two together by making these crackers in the shape of your favorite animals. If you don't have any animal cookie cutters, you can run to the grocery store to get some or just use the cutters you have.

What You'll Need

1/2 cup rolled oats

2 teaspoons honey

1/2 teaspoon salt

3/4 cup whole wheat flour

1/4 teaspoon baking soda

1/4 cup butter

1/4 cup buttermilk

1/8 teaspoon vanilla

1 teaspoon cinnamon

What to do

1. Preheat the oven to 400°F.

2. Place the oats in a blender, and spin them until they're ground to a fine flour. Place the ground oats in a large mixing bowl, and add the honey, salt, flour, and baking soda. Mix well.

3. Cut in the butter and then add buttermilk, vanilla, and cinnamon. Combine evenly.

4. Roll the dough out on a floured surface (your clean counter top will work just fine). Make sure the dough is thin and even. Then cut out with animal-shaped cookie cutters.

5. Place the cut pieces on an ungreased baking sheet and bake about 10 to 12 minutes, or until brown. Let cool on cooling racks and store in an airtight container.

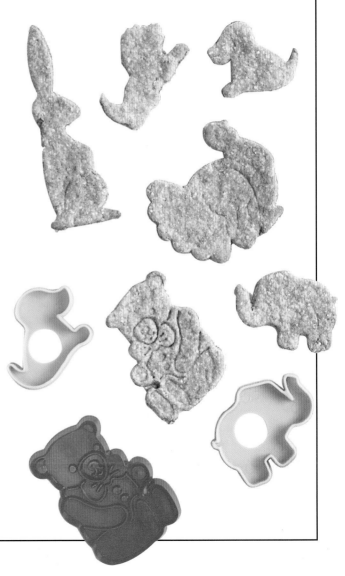

GORP

GORP stands for "Good Old Raisins and Peanuts"—a word used by backpackers who carry this light, nutritious mixture on long trips in the wilderness. We've added a little pizzazz to the traditional mix with chocolate chips or M&Ms. Ours makes a wonderful mix for a long road trip or a great midday snack. It takes only a couple minutes to make, but it will last a long time.

What You'll Need

1/3 pound shelled peanuts

1/3 pound raisins

1/8 pound chocolate chips or M&Ms

What to do

1. Mix everything in a large mixing bowl, and store the GORP in an airtight container.

Tip
Feel free to change the measurements to suit yourself.

Granola Bars

Granola alone is a wonderful snack but granola bars are a step toward snack heaven. Buying granola bars in the store can get pretty expensive, but now you can try them at home with your own choice of granola. If you like, use the granola recipe in this book!

What You'll Need

4-1/3 cups granola

1/8 teaspoon salt

1/4 cup honey

3 tablespoons molasses

1/4 teaspoon vanilla

1/8 teaspoon cinnamon

What to do

1. Preheat the oven to 350°F.

2. Stir everything together in a large mixing bowl. Make sure that it gets mixed well.

3. Line a small baking pan with waxed paper, and then grease the paper with margarine or shortening. Press the mixture into the baking pan, and bake for 12 to 15 minutes, until lightly browned.

4. Remove the granola from the oven, and let it cool for about 5 minutes. Turn the pan over (using pot holders), and remove the baked mixture from the pan. Peel off the waxed paper, and cut the granola into smaller bars.

Bob's Bogus Bread

Makes 2 loaves

Our friend Bob is a great guy and the ultimate bread baker. He bakes wonderful whole wheat bread, rye bread, sourdough bread, and fresh rolls. He's shared his best recipe with us, so jump into your bread-baking mood and check out the best bogus bread you'll ever taste.

What You'll Need

2 cups unbleached, all-purpose flour

2 envelopes quick-rise yeast

1/3 cup sugar

2 tablespoons salt

2 cups milk

1 egg

1/4 cup vegetable oil

2 to 3-1/2 cups whole wheat flour

What to do

1. Mix the all-purpose flour, yeast, sugar, and salt in a large mixing bowl.

2. Heat the milk in a microwave oven for 4 minutes, or heat it on the stove until it's warm to the touch. Add the milk to the dry mixture, and stir well. Add the egg and oil. Beat on high for 3 minutes with an electric mixer, or stir quickly and well for 5 minutes.

3. Add 2 cups of the whole wheat flour, and mix well. Add additional flour (up to a total of 3-1/2 cups) until the mixture is stiff and cleans the sides of the bowl.

4. Dump onto a floured surface and knead for about 4 minutes. Then wash and dry your mixing bowl, and spread a drop of oil around in it. Place the dough in the bowl and cover with a towel for 10 minutes.

5. Remove the dough from the bowl and knead again for about 5 minutes, removing all the large air bubbles. Divide and place in two lightly greased bread pans. Allow the loaves to rise for about 40 minutes.

6. Preheat oven to 375°F. Bake the loaves for 25 to 30 minutes. They are ready when they sound hollow when tapped on the bottom. Let them sit on cooling racks until completely cooled. You should give them about 5 hours to cool—if you can wait that long.

Fruit and Vegetable Snacks

Sunshine Seen Between

3 to 5 Servings

You can make this snack for a school group or a small party. Everyone seems to like this simple and quick recipe. It's also easy to make just a few for yourself, using one banana.

What You'll Need

2 bananas

28 vanilla wafers

What to do

1. Peel both bananas completely.

2. Cut each banana into seven thick coins.

3. Use the vanilla wafers to make sandwiches, with a banana coin between two vanilla wafers. Look and see the "sunshine" between the wafers. YUM.

Summer Special

This is a great snack to take when you go hiking. When you stop to rest on top of a mountain or at the bottom of a waterfall, try a summer special!

What You'll Need

2 leaves of cabbage, about the same size

1/3 cup peanut butter

1/4 cup raisins

What to do

1. Wash the cabbage leaves under running water.

2. Spread all the peanut butter on one side of one leaf with a rubber spatula. Sprinkle the raisins on the peanut butter.

3. Place the other leaf on the peanut butter and raisins, making a sandwich.

4. Cut the sandwich into smaller pieces. You might like to make funny shapes with your sandwich cuttings.

Tip
You can also add raisins, granola, peanuts, sunflower seeds, or pumpkin seeds, along with the peanut butter

Fruit and Vegetable Snacks 39

Chunky Applesauce

This applesauce originated deep in the Blue Ridge Mountains and is so good we were inspired to share it with you. Our recipe uses the microwave to keep the freshness of the delicious apples in the sauce, instead of boiling away all the nutrition and taste.

What You'll Need

2 McIntosh apples

2 Granny Smith apples

1-1/2 cups water

2 tablespoons fresh lemon juice

1/2 cup brown sugar

1 teaspoon cinnamon

1/4 teaspoon nutmeg

What to do

1. Core the apples, and then halve them. Cut each half into small chunks.

2. Combine the apples, water, and lemon juice in a microwave-safe bowl.

3. Stir the sugar, cinnamon, and nutmeg together in a soup-size bowl, and combine them with the apple mixture. Cook uncovered for 5 minutes at full power.

4. Stir the apples, pressing them into the liquid, and then cook for 5 more minutes, or until the apples are cooked. (Remember, this is chunky applesauce, so you will have chunks of apples in your sauce.)

5. With a potato masher, mash the apples with the liquid.

6. Allow the applesauce to cool to room temperature. If you like your applesauce cold, cover it and put it in the refrigerator before serving.

Fruit Skewers

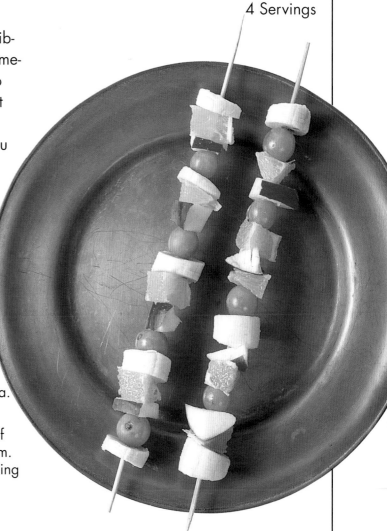

4 Servings

Wow! This is a wonderful idea for nibbling on while you're doing your homework. It takes almost no time at all to make, and it lasts for a while. It's not important that you use just our fruit ideas. If you find a fresh fruit that you want to use instead, go ahead!

What You'll Need

1 banana

1 apple

1 orange

10 grapes

4 wooden skewers

What to do

1. Peel the orange and the banana.

2. Cut the apple carefully with a sharp knife into chunks about the size of your nose. Don't use the core or the stem. Place the chunks in a medium-sized mixing bowl.

3. Cut the orange into chunks the same size, and add them to the apples. Slice the banana into thick coins, and add those to the apples and oranges.

4. Add the grapes to the other fruit.

5. Stick the fruit on the skewers. Mix the fruit pattern on each skewer to make it interesting.

6. Eat by simply sliding the fruit off the skewer and into your mouth!

Tip
A little lemon juice drizzled on the fruit keeps it from turning brown (but it also makes the fruit taste sour).

Cucumber Sandwich

1 Serving

Wake up your mouth with a cool, fresh cucumber sandwich made with alfalfa sprouts and cream cheese. These are great for your lunch box.

What You'll Need

2 slices of bread

1 medium cucumber

1/4 cup cream cheese

1/3 cup alfalfa sprouts

What to do

1. Rinse the cucumber under running water, and then cut it into thick coins.

2. Spread the cream cheese on the bread with a butter knife. Add the cucumber coins and alfalfa sprouts, then add the other slice of bread.

Hummus

Makes 3 cups (about 8 servings)

Hummus (say HUM-us) is probably the most famous dish from the Middle East. It's a wonderful dip for raw vegetables and a terrific sandwich spread (add alfalfa sprouts or cucumber coins to your sandwich, if you wish). It's also great to spread on crackers or pita chips (see the recipe on page 29).

What You'll Need

1 can cooked chick-peas (also called garbanzo beans)

3/4 cup tahini*

3/4 cup freshly squeezed lemon juice

1 teaspoon chopped garlic

1 teaspoon salt

Pinch cayenne pepper (if you wish)

What to do

1. Drain the chick-peas.

2. Get an adult to help you with this step. Place all the ingredients in a food processor or blender, and process until well mixed. Add a little water, about a table-spoonful at a time, until you have a smooth, creamy mixture.

3. Taste the hummus, and if it needs anything more—lemon juice, tahini, or gar-lic—add it and process the mixture again.

*Tahini (tah-HEE-nee) is made of sesame seeds that have been ground into a paste. It's available in the ethnic-foods section of most grocery stores and in health-food stores.

Fruit Festival

Fruit is one of the most refreshing foods, and one of the most colorful when different kinds are put together. We celebrate fruit with this recipe, which combines the coolness of fruit and the crunch of nuts. Serve some up to all your pals and have a festival. Enjoy!

dew, grapefruit, watermelon, peaches, nectarines, pears, blueberries, raspberries, strawberries, pineapple, and kiwi.

Tip

You can mix the salad with cottage cheese instead of yogurt, if you'd rather.

What You'll Need

1 apple

1 banana

1 orange

Other seasonal fruits*

1 tablespoon fresh lemon juice

1/2 cup walnuts or pecans

1 cup vanilla yogurt

What to do

1. Peel both the banana and the orange.

2. Cut the apple, banana, and orange into pieces about the size of your nose, and put them in a large mixing bowl.

3. Pour the lemon juice on the fruit and mix carefully. The lemon juice keeps the fruit from turning brown.

4. Chop the nuts into pieces about the size of your thumbnail, and add them to the fruit mixture.

5. Add the yogurt, and mix carefully again.

*See which fruits are in season at your grocery store. These fruits are super for adding to a fruit salad: cantaloupe, honey-

Banana Pops

Banana pops combine a sweet, soft banana with yummy, crunchy wheat germ or granola. Eat these just like frozen pops but enjoy them much more! You can also place one in the freezer to eat later.

What You'll Need

1 banana

2 tablespoons honey

1/4 cup wheat germ or granola

2 popsicle sticks

What to do

1. Peel the banana and cut it in half, crosswise.

2. Push a popsicle stick into the cut end of each banana half, about an inch deep.

3. With a rubber spatula, spread honey over the surface of the banana.

4. Put wheat germ or granola in a small bowl, and roll the honey-covered banana in it until the banana is covered.

The Greater Mater

1 Serving

More people grow tomatoes in their backyard gardens than any other crop. And no wonder! Nothing tastes better. This recipe is good with any tomato— large or small, round or pear-shaped, red or yellow.

What You'll Need

1 large tomato

1/3 cup cottage cheese

(continued on next page)

What to do

1. Slice off the very top of the tomato, and scoop out the seeds and pulp with a spoon.

2. Fill with cottage cheese and eat! YUM!

Tip

Sprinkle chopped nuts on top for crunch, or stuff the tomato with hummus (see the recipe on page 42) instead of cottage cheese.

Apple Volcanoes

These can get totally messy, but the best part is the yummy peanut butter waiting inside, ready to erupt with taste! Try them with other fillings and toppings to make them even more interesting.

What You'll Need

1 apple
1/2 cup peanut butter
1/4 cup sunflower seeds

What to do

1. Core the apple with an apple corer. If you don't have that tool, get a grown-up to help you core the apple with a knife.

2. Fill the hole of the apple with the peanut butter. A butter knife works well for this.

3. Sprinkle the sunflower seeds on the peanut butter, and let the volcano erupt with taste in your mouth.

The Other Volcanoes

Under the Earth's surface there is hot melted rock, called magma, which is always moving. It's like a stew simmering beneath the Earth's crust. When the magma finds a weak or broken spot in the crust above it, it breaks through the surface, spitting out the magma. This is called a volcano.

Celery Stuffers

Celery stuffers are wonderful with a cold glass of milk. Use your imagination to make new stuffings or super toppings. Feel free to add to or change the recipes to your liking. You can always place some in the refrigerator to eat later.

What You'll Need

2 large celery stalks (with leaves)

1/4 cup cream cheese

2 tablespoons sunflower seeds

10 to 15 raisins

1 tablespoon honey

What to do

1. Carefully rub the celery under running water to clean it. Cut off about an inch of each stalk on the big, tough end.

2. Use a butter knife to fill the hollows with the cream cheese.

3. Place the raisins on top of the cream cheese, pushing them into the cream cheese a little so they won't fall off. Sprinkle the seeds on top.

4. Drizzle the honey over the stuffed celery, and voila!

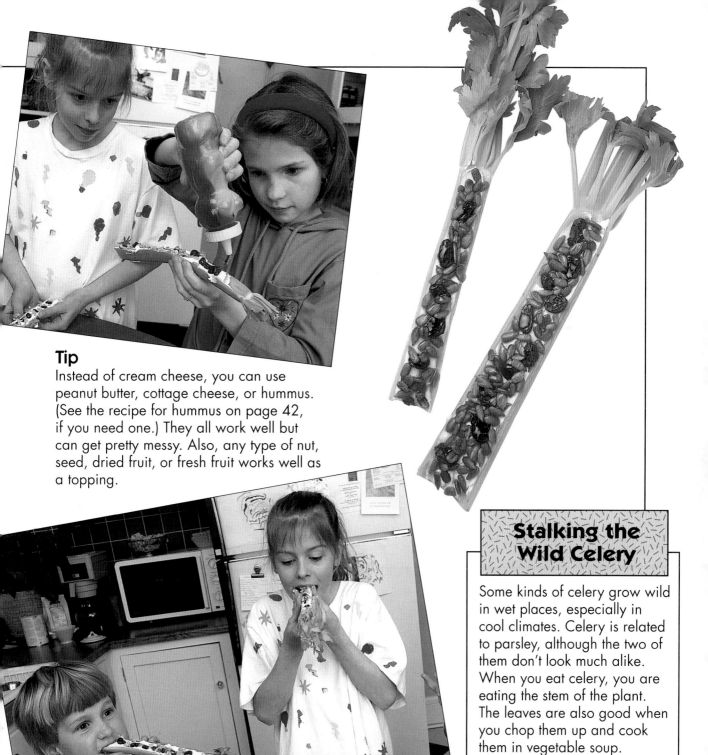

Tip

Instead of cream cheese, you can use peanut butter, cottage cheese, or hummus. (See the recipe for hummus on page 42, if you need one.) They all work well but can get pretty messy. Also, any type of nut, seed, dried fruit, or fresh fruit works well as a topping.

Stalking the Wild Celery

Some kinds of celery grow wild in wet places, especially in cool climates. Celery is related to parsley, although the two of them don't look much alike. When you eat celery, you are eating the stem of the plant. The leaves are also good when you chop them up and cook them in vegetable soup.

Fruit and Vegetable Snacks 49

Salad People

Are you interested in making small stick-figures of people? If so, this recipe is for you. Be creative with your people by adding more parts or changing some of them. Try making one that looks like you or your mom.

What You'll Need

1 carrot, cut into sticks

1 small cucumber, sliced into thick coins

4 grapes

1 lettuce leaf

8 raisins

What to do

1. Assemble all the pieces to look like people: a cucumber body, a grape head, carrot stick arms and legs, lettuce hair, raisin buttons, and so on. Now eat your people.

Applesauce Surprise

1 Serving

Now that you can make great applesauce from the recipe on page 40, you're ready to add some treats to it. This is an easy little snack to make for yourself anytime. Surprise!

What You'll Need

2 cups natural applesauce*

1/2 teaspoon ground cinnamon

1/4 cup raisins

What to do

1. Place the applesauce in a soup-size bowl.

2. Sprinkle the cinnamon on the applesauce.

3. Place the raisins on top of the applesauce.

4. Surprise! Look what you can do with applesauce!

*You can also use some other kind of fruit sauce.

Isaac Newton's Apple

Has anyone ever told you about Isaac Newton sitting on a bench in his garden and seeing an apple fall from an apple tree? The story goes that he wondered what allowed that apple to fall and invented the theory of gravity on the spot. Actually, the whole story is just a myth...so don't believe it.

Hearty Foods

Lotsa Pasta

4 Servings

Here's a new twist to an old idea. We've added some fun and yummy ingredients to pasta salad. Serve your family or friends, because there's plenty of Lotsa Pasta.

What You'll Need

- 1/2 pound pasta, cooked and drained*
- 2 tablespoons of your favorite salad dressing
- 1 medium carrot, cut into thin coins
- 1 celery stalk, sliced
- 1/2 green bell pepper, cut into short strips
- 1/2 tomato, diced
- 2 ounces of your favorite cheese

What to do

1. In a large mixing bowl, toss the pasta with the salad dressing and then with all the other ingredients.

2. Let the salad sit for at least 1/2 hour, so that all the flavors can combine.

*Don't use long noodles, like spaghetti. Instead, use bow ties, spirals, or other short noodles.

Tip

You can change the vegetables according to your taste. Just remember that the best pasta salads are made with many different colors, so don't use all green vegetables.

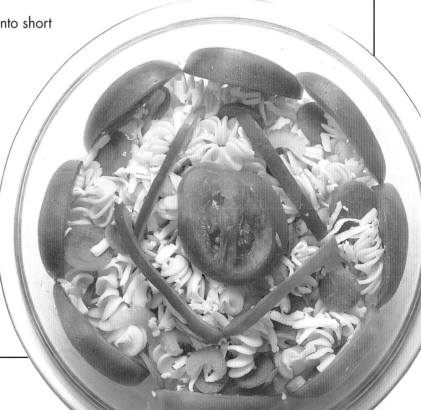

Veggie Soup

4 Servings

If you ever get a cold, this is the way to cure it (or so they say), but even if you don't have a cold, you can still enjoy this warm, homemade vegetable soup. If you like other veggies, just add them to the pot.

What You'll Need

2 carrots

2 celery stalks

1 potato

1 green pepper

1/2 medium onion

2-1/2 cups water

2 cups tomato juice

2 bouillon cubes

1/4 cup butter

What to do

1. Wash the carrots and celery, and slice them into thin coins. Cut the green pepper into small pieces and the potato into medium chunks. Chop the onion into medium pieces.

2. Put everything in a large pot and bring to a boil, then simmer for 30 minutes.

3. Add the bouillon cubes and butter. Simmer for 30 more minutes and eat!

Sizzling Open-Faced Sandwich

1 Serving

What a wonderful idea for a hearty personal dinner! Maybe you'd like to share it with a friend or an adult. You might even want to share it with your babysitter. Open-faced sandwiches are super for an empty stomach.

What You'll Need

1 slice of bread

Butter or margarine

1/4 apple

2 slices of your favorite cheese

1/4 cup cashews, walnuts, or peanuts

What to do

1. Butter the bread.

2. Cut the apple in thin slices, and place the slices on the buttered side of the bread.

3. Cover the apple slices with the cheese slices, then sprinkle the nuts on top.

4. Broil under low heat until the nuts are lightly browned and the cheese bubbles.

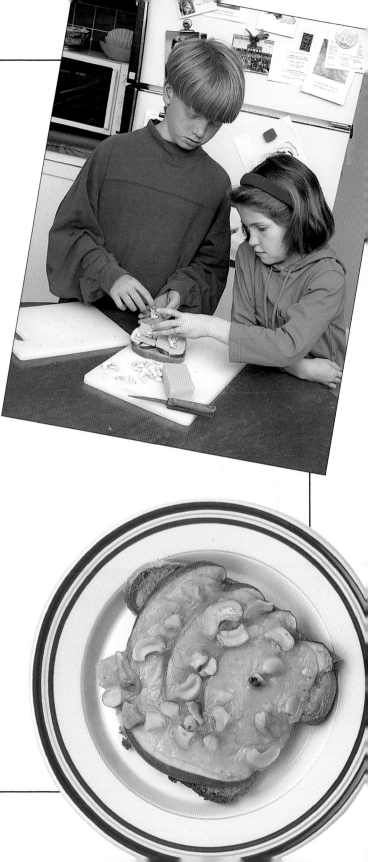

Variations

- Add raisins to the nuts.
- Use a banana instead of an apple.
- Use two different types of cheese.

Garden Salad

1, 2, or 3 Servings

This is a true garden harvest of fresh vegetables and greens that everyone—and we mean everyone—will love. You could share it with your family at dinner, along with some fresh bread. Or, if you're really hungry, you could eat the whole bowl-full yourself!

What You'll Need

2 large handfuls of lettuce

1 small handful of spinach

1/2 cucumber

1 large carrot

1 stalk celery

1/2 tomato

1/2 green pepper

What to do

1. Rinse off everything under running water. Do not scrub the vegetables, just rub them lightly with your fingers to clean them.

2. Tear the lettuce and spinach into bite-sized pieces, and put them into a large mixing bowl.

3. If you want to peel the cucumber and carrot, go ahead. Otherwise, just slice them and the celery into thick coins, and add them to the bowl.

4. Cut the tomato half into small chunks, and place those in the bowl. Cut the green pepper into thin strips, and put them in the bowl too.

5. Gently toss the salad with two wooden spoons, and serve. Use your favorite salad dressing, and eat up!

Personal Muffin Pizzas

Our personal muffin pizzas are made with English muffins, but if you like French bread, biscuits, or regular bread, those are perfectly fine, too. Your tastes may not always be like ours, so you are allowed to change or add to your pizza.

What You'll Need

1 English muffin

1/2 cup tomato pizza sauce

1 cup grated cheese (mozzarella, cheddar, etc)

What to do

1. Preheat the oven to 275°F.

2. Separate the English muffin into two halves.

3. Spread half of the sauce on one muffin piece and half on the other, using a table knife or a rubber spatula.

4. Sprinkle the grated cheese on the top so that it covers all the sauce.

5. Add any extra toppings you like. These are all good: green peppers, olives, onions, tomatoes, broccoli, pineapple, mushrooms, and corn kernels.

6. Place the pizzas in the oven until the cheese has melted and browned slightly.

Pizza

Pizza was invented in Naples, Italy, by some hungry, hard-working women while they waited for their bread dough to rise and bake. They took pieces of dough, flattened them (so they would bake fast), and sprinkled them with the seasonings that were lying around. Then they quickly baked the dough and ate it!

Humpty Dumpty Yummies

Egg salad sandwiches of all sorts can be found all over the world at picnics, cookouts, and dinner or lunch parties. It's a simple kid's favorite, and a grown-up favorite too. If you don't like eggs, try using tofu instead.

What You'll Need

- 2 hard-boiled eggs
- 1 celery stalk, sliced thinly
- 1/4 cup mayonnaise
- 3 lettuce leaves
- 3 slices tomato
- 6 slices bread

What to do

1. Peel the eggs and place them in a medium-sized bowl. Squish them with a fork.

2. Add the celery and mayonnaise, and mix well.

3. Put one slice of tomato and one lettuce leaf on each sandwich, and add as much egg salad as you want

Tuna Melt

1 Serving

A big tuna melt always satisfies your hunger and always tastes good.

What You'll Need

1 6-ounce can tuna packed in water

1/4 cup mayonnaise

1 slice bread

1 cup grated cheese

What to do

1. Drain the tuna by pressing the top of the can down on the tuna, turning it upside down over the sink, and allowing the liquid to drain out.

2. Mix the tuna and mayonnaise in a soup-size bowl.

3. Put as much tuna as you like on the slice of bread and cover it with cheese.

4. Broil until the cheese bubbles and browns lightly.

Chili

Chili is a super-duper, killer-diller, feel-good food. It seems to make everyone feel better. If you have any left over, freeze it for later. Then, some cool night, you can defrost your chili and have a warm and spicy meal that nobody ever turns down.

What You'll Need

2 tablespoons olive oil

2 onions, chopped

1 green pepper, chopped

1 clove garlic, chopped

1/2 cup tomato paste

1 teaspoon ground black pepper

1 teaspoon ground cumin

1-1/2 teaspoons oregano

1 teaspoon salt

1 tablespoon dried basil

2 cups canned tomatoes

3 cups cooked or canned kidney beans

1 cup cooked or canned pinto beans

What to do

1. Heat the oil in a large pot. Add the onions, green pepper, and garlic, and cook for a couple of minutes. Add the tomato paste, black pepper, cumin, oregano, salt, and basil, and stir.

2. Add the tomatoes and beans, and cover the pot. Simmer for about 20 minutes, stirring every once in a while.

3. Taste and see if you need more seasoning, or if it needs to cook longer. If not, just enjoy!

Crying Eyes

When you cut up onions, do your eyes water and burn? If so, try one or two of these popular tips, and see if they help.

1. Put the onion in the refrigerator so that it's cold when you slice it.

2. Wear safety goggles.

3. Hold the onion under running water while you peel at. At least your eyes won't burn for that part of the job.

Twice-Baked Potatoes

4 Servings

Baked potatoes are good, but when they've been baked two times, they are wonderful. Add anything you want, and see how great they can be!

What You'll Need

2 potatoes

1/2 stick of butter

1 cup milk (or more, as needed)

1 teaspoon salt

1 teaspoon pepper

1-1/2 cups grated cheddar cheese

3 tablespoons parmesan cheese

What to do

1. Bake the potatoes in the oven or microwave. In a regular oven, bake them at 425°F for 1 hour. In a microwave, bake them on high for 5 or 6 minutes. (If you microwave them, be sure to poke a few holes in the skins with a fork so they don't explode.) When the time is up, pierce them with a fork to check for doneness. The fork should go in easily.

2. Cut each potato in half, and remove the insides from the skins with a spoon.

3. Place the insides in a large mixing bowl, and add the butter. Then mash with a fork or potato masher.

4. Add the milk, and whip with a whisk or electric mixer until fluffy. Then add salt, pepper, and half the grated cheddar.

5. Stuff the skins with the potato mixture, and top with the rest of the cheddar and the parmesan. Bake until the cheese melts. If you wish, you can then broil the potatoes for a few minutes to lightly brown the top.

Spicy Tofu

Wowzers! What an extraordinary idea! This recipe is a total knock-out for dinner, even if you think you won't like tofu. Believe me, everyone will like it, and you'll find yourself making a lot.

What You'll Need

1 pound tofu cut into rectangles (about 1 inch by 1-1/2 inches by 1/2 inch)

1/4 cup oil (olive, safflower, or canola)

1/4 cup soy sauce

1 tablespoon vinegar

1 tablespoon lemon juice

2 cloves garlic, minced

1/2 teaspoon basil

1/4 teaspoon thyme

1/4 teaspoon oregano

1/4 teaspoon powdered ginger or 1/2 teaspoon minced fresh ginger

1/8 teaspoon black pepper

What to do

1. Mix all the ingredients except the tofu in an ovenproof dish. Put the tofu rectangles in the pan, turning them over so they get fully covered, and lay them in the pan without overlapping.

2. Place the pan in the oven, and broil the tofu until it turns slightly brown. Turn the tofu over and repeat on the other side. Serve with rice or stir-fried vegetables.

Where To, Tofu?

Tofu ("toe-foo") is made from soybeans. It is most often eaten in China, Japan, and Korea. Many vegetarians—people who don't eat meat—eat tofu because it has lots of protein.

Vegetable Shish-Kebab

Fresh vegetables are perhaps the best source of nutrients, plus they taste so wonderful! This recipe uses all vegetables instead of meat, and it's guaranteed to become an all-time favorite.

Marinating involved! Make sure you plan ahead by about 4 hours.

What You'll Need

2 cups of your favorite salad dressing

3 zucchinis or yellow squash, cut into thick coins

5 medium tomatoes, quartered

12 medium mushrooms

1/2 small eggplant, cut into 1-1/2-inch chunks

2 medium green peppers, cut into strips

2 medium onions, cut into 1-1/2-inch chunks

Wooden or metal skewers

What to do

1. Pour the salad dressing into a large mixing bowl. Add all the vegetables and stir to coat them.

2. Cover the bowl with plastic wrap, and place it in the refrigerator for about 3 hours. If you're using wooden skewers, put them in water to soak (so they won't burn while you cook).

3. When you're ready to cook, stick the skewers through the vegetables, mixing the order from one skewer to the next to make them look interesting. Place them on a broiling pan or two.

4. Broil in the oven until golden brown. Make sure you turn over the skewers every few minutes to get every side done.

Tip

If a grown-up friend or relative is cooking out on the backyard grill, make some veggie shish-kebabs to add to the grill. The smoky taste of grilled veggies is wonderful!

Bean Burrito

2 Servings

Burritos with beans are special and tasty, not to mention doing wonders for your body. Share one with your friend and join him or her for the best burrito you'll ever eat.

What You'll Need

1 cup cooked or canned pinto beans

1 handful of lettuce

2 large flour tortillas

1/4 onion, chopped

1-1/2 cups grated cheddar cheese

1/2 tomato, chopped

1/2 cup sour cream

1/4 cup salsa or picante sauce

What to do

1. Preheat the oven to 300°F.

2. Drain the beans, and tear the lettuce into small pieces that can fit in your mouth.

3. Soften the tortillas in the microwave. To do that, sandwich the tortillas between two dampened paper towels, and microwave on full power for 10 seconds.

4. Put a couple of spoonfuls of beans in the middle of each tortilla, and sprinkle some onions on the beans.

5. Roll the tortilla up, and place it on a baking sheet. Sprinkle the cheese on top of the tortilla, and cover with aluminum foil.

6. Heat in the oven until the cheese melts (10 or 15 minutes). (Or microwave on high until the cheese melts and the burrito is hot.) Sprinkle the hot burrito with chopped onions, lettuce, and tomato. Serve with sour cream and salsa or picante sauce.

Mr. Fetti's Spaghetti

Mr. Fetti is an old man who lives in the hills of North Carolina. He lives with his three dogs and a horse on a beautiful piece of land. Every Wednesday night he makes his favorite spaghetti, and now he's letting you in on his special recipe.

What You'll Need

1-pound package spaghetti

1 teaspoon olive oil

1/2 medium onion, minced

2 15-ounce cans tomato sauce

1 16-ounce can whole tomatoes

1 6-ounce can tomato paste

1 tablespoon oregano

1 teaspoon basil

1 teaspoon garlic powder

1 teaspoon ground black pepper

Parmesan cheese

What to do

1. Heat the olive oil in a frying pan, add the onions, and cook for a few minutes.

2. Put the onions, all the tomato stuff, and the seasonings together in a large pot, and cook over low heat. Stir it every few minutes and watch it closely, because it burns easily. Simmer the sauce for about 15 minutes.

3. Fill another large pot a little over halfway full of water, and place it over high heat until it boils. Put the noodles in the pot, reduce the heat to medium-high, and boil until the noodles are soft (about 8 to 10 minutes). Keep the water boiling all during cooking, or the spaghetti will stick together.

4. When the noodles are ready, put them on a plate and top with the sauce. Sprinkle a little parmesan cheese on top.

DRINKS

Ice-Cubed Fruit

Makes 16

Put these ice cubes in your drink, and let them melt to release a juicy piece of fruit—a wonderful surprise at the bottom of the glass!

What You'll Need

16 grapes, raspberries, blueberries, cherries, small strawberries, or thin banana coins

Water

What to do

1. Fill an ice-cube tray with water, and place one piece of fruit in each hollow.

2. Place in the freezer, and allow to freeze completely.

3. When the ice cubes are frozen, serve them in any fruit drink.

Shake, Rattle, and Roll!

Shakes have become so much fun that everybody can make up a list of new things to add! Here's a list or our favorite thick shakes.

What You'll Need

Nut and Honey:

    2 cups low-fat milk

    1/4 cup plain yogurt

    1/4 cup peanut butter

    2 teaspoons honey

More Bananas?

    1-1/2 cups low-fat milk

    1-1/2 bananas

    2 teaspoons vanilla extract

    1/4 teaspoon allspice

Rich Fruit Shake:

    1/2 cup sliced fruit (strawberries, banana, peaches, blueberries, cantaloupe, or other)

    1/3 cup apple juice

    1/2 cup crushed ice

    3/4 cup low-fat milk

Each recipe makes 2 servings

What to do

1. Put all the ingredients in a blender or processor fitted with a steel blade, and whip until thick and smooth.

2. Serve chilled.

Juice Spritzers

2 Servings

These spritzers are good for drinking with a friend or perfect for an after-school refresher.

What You'll Need

1-1/2 cups club soda or seltzer water

2 cups fruit juice of your choice

What to do

1. Combine the club soda or seltzer water with the fruit juice in a pitcher.

2. Pour the mixture into two glasses, and add ice if you wish.

3. It is also refreshing to add a thin slice of lemon or a couple of fresh mint leaves on top.

Lemonade

2 or 3 Servings

This tangy drink was first discovered in Paris, France, during the 1600s. It is just as easy to make your own lemonade as it is to mix up a frozen concentrate. Homemade lemonade is so much better, too!

(continued on next page)

What You'll Need

3 tablespoons honey

1 cup warm water

1/2 cup fresh lemon juice
(about 3 lemons)

2 cups cold water

1/2 extra lemon (optional)

1/2 orange (optional)

What to do

1. In a pot, dissolve the honey in the warm water, then add the lemon juice and cold water. Stir everything together.

2. Serve chilled.

3. If you want to, you can cut thin slices of lemons or oranges and let them float on top of the lemonade. They look neat.

Vegetable Kick

6 Servings

This is pretty close to the store-bought brand of vegetable juice, but making it at home with fresh vegetables is so much tastier and healthier. Add or change the vegetables if you don't like these ideas, because there are plenty of vegetables that taste very good when made into juice.

What You'll Need

4 cups tomato juice

2 leaves cabbage, chopped

2 leaves spinach

1 sprig parsley

1 stalk celery with leaves

1/2 small carrot

1 tablespoon lemon juice

1/4 teaspoon pepper

1/4 teaspoon basil

What to do

1. Place all the ingredients in a blender, and spin them until smooth. Serve chilled or over ice.

Mulled Apple Cider

Makes 1 Quart

There's nothing like hot apple cider with spices in it! It warms up your bod and your disposition.

What You'll Need

1 quart natural apple cider

3 cinnamon sticks

1 orange

1/8 teaspoon ground nutmeg

1/4 teaspoon ground cinnamon

1 tablespoon whole cloves

What to do

1. Cut up half the orange into thin slices, and save the other half to eat later.

2. Put all the ingredients in a large pot, and simmer them over low heat for about 20 minutes. You can keep the cider warm over very low heat for several hours.

3. Use a ladle to spoon the cider into 4 cups. Do not pour directly from the pot.

Watermelon Galore

2 Servings

When you think of fruit juice, you almost never think about watermelon, do you? Well, now you can. Enjoy the full flavor of that big fruit in one small glass.

What You'll Need

1/4 small watermelon

1 cup apple juice

1 tablespoon honey

What to do

1. Cut the watermelon into small chunks, and remove the seeds and the rind.

2. Puree the chunks, juice, and honey in a blender or processor until smooth.

Sunshine Tea

Makes 1 Quart

How is good iced tea made? We believe the best tea is made by the sun. Try filling a jar with water, adding some tea, and setting it in the sun for an afternoon. Check out what happens. Believe us, it's so good!

What You'll Need

2 large teabags, 4 small teabags, or 3 teaballs full of your favorite tea

1-quart glass jar, full of water

What to do

1. Place the teabags or teaballs in the water, screw a lid on it, and place in the sun for at least 4 hours.

2. Remove the teabags or teaballs from the water, and place the tea in the refrigerator—ready to drink.

Your Place or Mine?

In the early days, children were not allowed to sit at the dinner table with the grown-ups. Instead, they sat behind their parents, waiting for whatever food was passed back to them. Nowadays our parents are happy to have us sit with them at mealtime (well, at least most of us). Aren't you glad things have changed?

Fruit Smoothie

Fruit smoothies are wonderfully cool and sweet, and very easy to make.

What You'll Need

> 1 cup fresh strawberries
>
> 1 cup banana coins
>
> 1 kiwi, peeled and sliced
>
> 1/4 apple, cored, peeled, and sliced
>
> 1 cup fresh blueberries
>
> 1 cup apple juice

What to do

1. Puree everything in a blender until smooth, and pour into glasses to drink.

Party Punch

How can you get more exciting than this? This is the ultimate punch—even your grandparents will like it! Serve it to them and see. It's an unbeatable party hit!

What You'll Need

2 cups orange juice

2 cups apple juice

1 cup grape juice

1 cup seltzer water

What to do

1. Combine all the juices in a pitcher.

2. Right before serving, add the seltzer water.

Fruit Crisp

6 Servings

The special part of this recipe is that you can mix the fruits however you want to. If you like peaches with apples or apples with rhubarb, go ahead and mix them. Just be sure you use the right amount of fruit. Enjoy!

What You'll Need

6 cups sliced peaches, apples, or sweetened rhubarb

1/2 lemon

1 cup whole wheat flour

1 cup brown sugar

1/2 cup butter or margarine

1/2 cup broken nuts (cashews, pecans, or walnuts)

1/2 cup sunflower seeds

2 teaspoons cinnamon

1 teaspoon nutmeg

What to do

1. Preheat the oven to 375°F.

2. Grease two small baking pans with butter or margarine.

3. Place the fruit evenly in the baking pans, and sprinkle a little bit of lemon juice on top, to keep the fruit from turning brown.

4. With clean hands, crumble and mix the rest of the ingredients together in a medium-sized mixing bowl. (The topping should be lumpy, not smooth.) Spread the topping on the fruit with a rubber spatula.

5. Place in the oven for about 1/2 hour, until the top is browned. Let it cool a little and serve with vanilla ice cream or a little milk or cream.

Baked Apples

Apples and cinnamon couldn't taste any better than this! Here is the ultimate baked-apple recipe, so make some when it's cold outside—or any other time you're craving a hot apple.

What You'll Need

4 large apples

1/4 cup wheat germ

1/4 cup raisins

2 tablespoons sunflower seeds

2 tablespoons chopped walnuts

Juice from 1/2 lemon

1/4 teaspoon cinnamon

1 tablespoon brown sugar

1/8 teaspoon salt

1 tablespoon flour

3/4 cup apple juice

What to do

1. Preheat the oven to 350°F.

2. Core the apples, and place them in a greased baking dish that has a cover. Try to keep the apples close together in the pan.

3. Mix the wheat germ, raisins, seeds, nuts, lemon juice, cinnamon, sugar, and salt in a medium-sized mixing bowl.

4. Stuff the hollow of each apple with the mixture, using a spoon or a rubber spatula.

5. Mix the flour and apple juice in a small bowl, and pour some over each apple.

6. Bake the apples for about 40 minutes, covered. Let them cool a little before serving.

Poppy Seed Muffins

Poppy seed muffins are one of the most popular kinds of muffins because they are easy to make. Poppy seeds are very sweet and tasty, so the muffins are extra good. Try one when it's still warm from the oven.

What You'll Need

2-3/4 cups rolled oats

1/2 cup whole wheat flour

2-1/2 teaspoons baking powder

1/2 teaspoon salt

1/3 teaspoon nutmeg

2 eggs

2 tablespoons vegetable oil

1/4 cup honey

1-1/2 cup milk

2-1/2 tablespoons poppy seeds

1 teaspoon lemon juice

What to do

1. Preheat the oven to 375°F.

2. Grease a 12-cup muffin pan.

3. Place the oats in a blender, and spin them until they turn into a coarse flour. Make sure you put only 1/2 cup of oats in at a time. You will need only 2 cups of this oat flour for the recipe. If you have any left over after blending, throw it away.

4. Put oat flour in a medium-sized mixing bowl, and sift in wheat flour, baking powder, salt, and nutmeg.

5. Blend eggs, oil, and honey together in a blender, then pour them into a large mixing bowl.

6. Stir the milk, poppy seeds, and lemon juice into the egg-oil mixture. Add the dry ingredients to the liquid ones, stirring just enough to blend well.

7. Spoon the batter into muffin cups, filling each cup only 3/4 full, and bake for 15 minutes until lightly brown on top. Do not overcook!

Ginger's Cookies

There was once a small, pretty girl named Ginger who always had to walk a long way to school. Every morning she packed up her books and started off to the city. Her journey was very long, and it took her about 2 hours every day to get to school and back. One Sunday afternoon, when she was home, she decided to make some cookies that she could eat each morning as she walked to school. Ginger's special cookies were so good that they were named after her. Think about her when you're making these!

What You'll Need

3/4 cup butter

1 cup honey

2 eggs

1/3 cup molasses

3-1/2 cups whole wheat flour

2 tablespoons finely chopped fresh ginger

1-1/2 teaspoons baking soda

1-1/2 teaspoons cinnamon

1 teaspoon ground cloves

What to do

1. Preheat the oven to 350°F.

2. Grease a large baking sheet with butter or margarine.

3. Cream the 3/4 cup butter and the honey in a large mixing bowl, then add eggs and molasses and mix well.

4. Slowly add the flour, stirring as you do, so that it gets mixed well. It is very important that all flour clumps get broken

Makes about 2 Dozen

up. Add the rest of the ingredients next; be sure that everything is combined well.

5. Roll the dough on a clean, floured surface until it's about 1/4 inch thick. Cut it into shapes with a cookie cutter. Place them on the baking sheet, and bake them for about 10 minutes. You will probably have to do this step more than once for the amount of dough that you have.

6. When the cookies are done, cool them on racks before eating.

Just Jammin'

Makes 16

One of the authors—we won't say which one—once ate a bunch of these cookies that her mother had made for a fancy holiday party. Her mother had to make some more in a hurry and was not very happy about it. Her mother promised that if she wouldn't eat any of the second batch, she could have the recipe. Now you can have it too.

What You'll Need

8 tablespoons butter (1 stick), softened

1/2 cup sugar

1/2 teaspoon vanilla extract

1/2 teaspoon almond extract

1 egg, slightly beaten

1-1/2 cups all-purpose flour

1 teaspoon baking powder

1/4 teaspoon ground cloves

1/4 teaspoon nutmeg

1/4 teaspoon salt

1 cup raspberry, strawberry, or blackberry jam

(continued on next page)

What to do

1. Preheat the oven to 400°F.

2. Grease and lightly flour an 8-inch square baking pan. With an electric mixer, cream the butter, sugar, vanilla extract, and almond extract in a large mixing bowl.

3. Add the beaten egg to the butter mixture, and stir well.

4. Stir together all the dry ingredients in a medium-sized mixing bowl, and then add them to the butter mixture. Mix well.

5. Spread about half of the batter in the baking pan, and even it out with a rubber spatula. Cover the batter in the pan with a thick layer of the jam, using a rubber spatula.

6. Spread the rest of the batter on the jam carefully with a rubber spatula, and bake for about 25 minutes, until batter is lightly browned.

7. Let cool and cut into 16 squares.

Harvest Bars

Sometimes the dough for these bars tastes better straight from the bowl than from the oven. You might have to hide it from your family before it goes in the oven, or it might disappear.

What You'll Need

1 cup butter or margarine

3/4 cup white sugar

3/4 cup brown sugar

2 eggs

1-1/2 cups flour

1 teaspoon baking soda

1/2 teaspoon salt

1 teaspoon vanilla

3 cups rolled oats

1 cup chocolate chips

What to do

1. Preheat the oven to 350°F.

2. Grease a cookie sheet with sides, then cream the butter and both sugars in a large mixing bowl, using a fork or an electric mixer. Add the eggs and mix well.

3. Mix the flour with the baking soda and salt, then add them to the butter and sugar. Add vanilla to mixture, and mix well.

4. Stir in the oats and chocolate chips. Make sure that everything is combined evenly and the chips are spread out.

5. Spread the batter on a cookie sheet with a rubber spatula, and bake for 25 minutes. When ready, remove from the oven and let cool. When cool enough, cut into squares and eat!

Peanut Butter Balls

Makes about 2 Dozen

Peanut butter balls are wonderful! They are great for wrapping up and packing in your lunch or for snacking on after a meal.

What You'll Need

1/2 cup honey

1/2 cup peanut butter

3/4 cup powdered milk*

1/3 cup wheat germ

What to do

1. Blend honey, peanut butter, and powdered milk in a large mixing bowl.

2. Roll the mixture into balls about the size of a small marble. Roll each ball in wheat germ to cover fully.

3. Chill in the refrigerator for about 30 minutes, and eat up!

*Note: This is not evaporated milk! Powdered milk is a dry powder; evaporated milk is a liquid that comes in a can. Make sure you have powdered milk before you begin.

Tip

You can also add vanilla extract, chocolate chips, shredded coconut, raisins, sunflower seeds, or M&Ms. Use a little more peanut butter and honey if you do decide to add more stuff.

George Washington Carver

George Washington Carver experimented with many things in his lifetime. One of these things was the peanut. Carver found out that if he planted peanuts in the soil, the growing peanuts would improve the soil and farmers could grow bigger and better crops. Instead of wasting the peanuts that he grew, Carver invented many uses for them, such as cereals, oils, dyes, soaps, and food substitutes.

PB Glop

4 Servings

You will not believe how good PB Glop is until you try this recipe. Take a handful of it, and you'll find that it is super! It works great for camping and hiking, if you just put it in a hard container like a clean jar or can.

What You'll Need

- 1-1/4 cups peanut butter
- 3/4 cup honey
- 1 cup raisins
- 1 cup sunflower seeds
- 1/2 teaspoon vanilla extract
- 2-1/4 cups crisped rice cereal

What to do

1. Stir everything except the cereal together in a large mixing bowl.

2. Gently mix in the cereal.

3. Store in a hard container in the refrigerator.

Pumpkin Pie

One 9-inch Pie

Guess what! Pumpkins are not just for making jack-o'-lanterns on Halloween. They are very yummy and truly sweet, so they make number-one, A+, super-duper pies. You can eat them anytime, no matter what the season. Mmmmmm.

What You'll Need

- 1 9-inch frozen pie crust*
- 1-1/2 cups fresh or canned pumpkin puree
- 1/4 teaspoon salt
- 1/2 cup evaporated milk
- 2 eggs, beaten
- 1/2 cup molasses
- 2 tablespoons maple syrup
- 1 teaspoon cinnamon
- 1/3 teaspoon nutmeg
- 1/3 teaspoon ginger
- 1/2 teaspoon vanilla extract

*You can buy these at the grocery store.

What to do

1. Preheat the oven to 450°F.

2. Thaw the pie crust (read the label for directions). Mix all the rest of the ingredients in the order listed, in a large mixing bowl.

3. Pour the filling into the crust, and bake for about 15 minutes. Then turn the oven down to 350°, and bake for 40 minutes. If the middle is still juicy, the pie isn't ready; leave it in for about 5 more minutes and then check again.

Cut Twice, Eat Once

Any way you slice it, the first piece of a pie is fun to eat. But it's hard to get that first piece out of the pie without breaking it. To make it easier, go ahead and cut two pieces before you remove the first one. That extra cut makes the pie a little more flexible and less likely to break.

Patriotic Prize

3 Servings

This can be your Fourth of July treat or just a cure for your sweet tooth. The trick is to smother your ice cream with fruit and celebrate the red, white, and blue on your own plate. Make some for your friends or parents, and salute them with a smile!

What You'll Need

1/4 cup strawberry or raspberry preserves

1/4 cup cranberry, strawberry, or any other red berry juice

1/2 pint vanilla ice cream

1/2 cup fresh blueberries

1/4 cup fresh strawberries, sliced

What to do

1. In a small bowl, stir the preserves and the juice together until well mixed.*

2. Divide the ice cream into 3 bowls, and pour the berry sauce on top. Add the blueberries and strawberries, and you've got yourself a patriotic prize of American pride.

*You might want to heat the sauce up in the microwave for about 45 seconds.

Banana Boats

If you've ever seen a crew of rowers rowing together on a lake or river, you know how interesting it is to watch and how strong the crew is. Now you get to create your own crew.

What You'll Need

1 banana, cut lengthwise

1/4 cup peanut butter

12 raisins, berries, or chocolate chips

What to do

1. Spread the peanut butter on the flat side of both banana slices.

2. Place 6 raisins, berries, or chocolate chips on the peanut butter, to be the rowers of the boat.

Arctic Treats

10 Servings

Ice cream and frozen yogurt sandwiches are the ultimate party desserts, because they are so good and they are so messy! Have everybody make their own, then go outside and enjoy the fun. Remember that nobody can eat one and keep their face and hands clean!

What You'll Need

1 16-ounce box graham crackers

1/2-gallon carton ice cream

What to do

1. Cut a slice of ice cream widthwise, and place it between two graham crackers. That's it! Save leftover crackers and ice cream for later.

Tip

For a real mess, top your treat off with whipped cream and a strawberry!

Frozen Creamy Fruit

This treat is wonderful for a quick party snack. Make a few ice cube trays of it to share with all your friends. You may even ask them to help. It's fun and easy!

What You'll Need

2/3 cup evaporated milk

1 10-ounce package frozen, unsweetened fruit

1-1/2 tablespoons honey

12 toothpicks

What to do

1. Blend everything (except the toothpicks!) in a blender until it becomes thick and smooth.

2. Pour the mixture into an ice cube tray, and place it in the freezer until frozen.

3. When frozen, push tooth picks or popsicle sticks in the tops of the cubes and eat!

Fruit Pops

5 Servings

The fruitiest, juiciest, most refreshing sweet is a frozen fruit pop. It cools you down when you're hot and sweaty, and it fills you up when you're a little hungry. It's a great idea for summer treats to share with a couple of friends. One lick and you'll fall in love with fruit pops.

What You'll Need

1/2 banana

1 cup apple juice

1/2 cup strawberries, peaches, or raspberries

2 teaspoons fresh lemon juice

What to do

1. Puree all the ingredients in a blender.

2. Pour the mixture into popsicle containers or an ice cube tray, and place in the freezer until frozen.

Oatmeal Raisin Cookie

Just about any oatmeal raisin cookies are good, but these will blow you away! Try them and watch them disappear in minutes. You might want to make some to save just for yourself!

What You'll Need

1-1/2 cups quick-cooking rolled oats

3/4 cup unbleached all-purpose flour

1/2 teaspoon ground cinnamon

1/4 teaspoon ground cloves

1/8 teaspoon salt

1/2 teaspoon baking soda

8 tablespoons (1 stick) butter, at room temperature

1/2 cup packed brown sugar

1/2 cup white sugar

1 egg

1-1/4 teaspoons vanilla extract

1/2 cup raisins

What to do

1. Preheat the oven to 350°F.

2. Lightly grease two baking sheets.

3. Stir together the oats, flour, cinnamon, cloves, salt, and baking soda in a large mixing bowl.

4. Cream the butter and both sugars in another large mixing bowl until light and smooth. Beat in the eggs and vanilla with a whisk. Slowly mix in the oat-and-flour mixture, then the raisins.

5. Spoon the batter onto the baking sheets with a teaspoon, spacing them about 2 inches apart.

6. Bake for about 10 minutes, until golden brown.

7. Remove from the oven, and leave cookies on baking sheets for 3 to 4 minutes. Then remove the cookies and place on cooling racks.

Frozen Noses

These are fun to serve—especially when you tell people what they're called! They are very simple to make but need to sit in the freezer for a couple of hours.

What You'll Need

3 bananas

What to do

1. Grease two baking sheets.

2. Peel and cut each banana into four or five thick coins.

3. Place the banana chunks on the baking sheets, and put them in the freezer for at least 4 hours. Enjoy!

Tip

Try these in a bowl with milk and cinnamon.

Spicy Party Nuts

Makes 6 Cups

Go nuts with this! This recipe can be for any occasion, from a Thanksgiving family gathering to one of your biggest birthday parties. You might even like it so much that you make it when there's nothing to party about. Spicy party nuts make a great lunch box snack.

What You'll Need

4 cups mixed nuts

1 cup sunflower seeds

1/2 cup butter

1 teaspoon salt

2 teaspoons garlic powder

1/2 teaspoon cinnamon

2 teaspoons ground cumin

1-1/2 tablespoons curry powder

1 teaspoon cayenne pepper

2 cups shredded coconut, toasted

What to do

1. Saute the nuts and seeds in the butter in a frying pan over low heat, stirring constantly for about 5 minutes.

2. Add the salt, garlic powder, curry powder, cumin, and cayenne to the pan, and saute for about 2 more minutes. Add the coconut and stir a couple times to mix.

3. Remove the mixture from the heat, and let it cool. You still need to stir it often for about 30 minutes so the nuts and spices blend together well. Place the spiced nuts on paper towels for about 15 minutes, and then store them in an airtight container until serving time.

Tip
To toast coconut, spread it in a thin layer on a baking sheet, and bake it at 300°F for 5 to 10 minutes, or until it turns golden brown. Watch it carefully so it doesn't burn!

Guacamole

10 Servings

Your party guests will come back for more and more—and more!—of this spicy, chunky, fresh dip. It's perfect with warmed corn tortilla chips. Get a taste of Mexico when you eat some of this!

What You'll Need

4 ripe avocados

1 medium onion, chopped fine

1 clove garlic, chopped fine

1/2 teaspoon red chili powder

1/2 teaspoon salt

1/4 teaspoon pepper

1/2 teaspoon ground cumin

1 tablespoon fresh lemon juice

1/4 cup salsa or picante sauce

1-1/2 tomatoes, chopped

What to do

1. Mash the avocados in a large mixing bowl with a potato masher or fork. Add all the other ingredients except the tomato, and mix well.

2. Add tomatoes and stir gently. Serve with tortilla chips, and yummy!

Nachos Amigos!

About 10 Servings

Nachos taste good anytime for any occasion, so serve them up to all your buddies. The secret is to pile the chips with goodies. Enjoy!

What You'll Need

2 10-ounce bags corn tortilla chips

2 cans refried beans (refritos)

2 cups grated cheddar cheese

1 diced onion

2 diced tomatoes

1 cup sour cream

1/2 cup sliced black olives

What to do

1. Preheat the oven to 250°F.

2. Pour each bag of chips on one baking sheet, so that you have two baking sheets piled with chips.

3. Evenly add the beans, cheese, onions on top of the chips, and place them in the oven for 8 to 10 minutes.

4. Add everything else on the top right before you serve.

Traveling Cheese

There are over 200 varieties of cheese around the world. Most of them are made in France, Italy, Germany, Holland, Switzerland, Scandinavia, the British Isles, the United States, and Canada. Many cheeses are named for the place they were invented. Cheddar cheese was first made in England near a small town called Cheddar. Parmesan cheese was first made in Parma, Italy.

Salsa

Salsa is a great addition to chips or nachos, or just about anything that's missing a spicy kick. This recipe isn't super spicy, so if you like salsa that sizzles, add more green chiles. Try this salsa with the burrito on page 66 or with the egg recipe on page 17.

What You'll Need

4 large tomatoes

1/4 cup chopped onion

1/8 teaspoon red chili powder

1/2 4-ounce can chopped green chiles

3 tablespoons fresh minced parsley

2 tablespoons vinegar

1/2 teaspoon salt

1/4 teaspoon pepper

What to do

1. Puree all the ingredients in a food processor or blender. If you like chunky salsa, don't whip it for long.

2. Let the salsa sit for about 15 minutes before you serve it, so that the flavors combine well. Store it in an airtight jar in the refrigerator.

More Salsa

These days, salsa is one of the most popular foods around. Lots of people are using it instead of ketchup on burgers, and enjoying it with chips, as a salad dressing—with anything that needs an extra kick. Salsa is Spanish for "sauce." We all have our Mexican friends to thank for this terrific dish.

FUN KITCHEN PROJECTS & GIFTS

Honey Butter

6 to 8 Servings

Honey butter is wonderful on biscuits, coffeecake, cornbread, whole wheat bread, and scones. This recipe will make you jump head over heels, so make some for friends, and share with them the sweetness of honey.

Good Manners Aren't Everything

I eat my peas with honey.

I've done it all my life.

It makes the peas taste funny,

But it keeps them on my knife.

What You'll Need

1-1/2 cups margarine or butter

2 cups honey

What to do

1. Place butter and honey in a medium-sized mixing bowl.

2. Using an electric mixer, beat ingredients until smooth.

3. Store the honey butter in the refrigerator when it's not being used. Beat it again if it separates later.

Strawberry Pancake Syrup

Makes 1-1/2 Cups

Pancake syrups are probably one of the greatest gifts you could ever make. This one is so sweet and delicious I promise just about anyone will enjoy it. Try decorating the bottle with ribbons and flowers so it looks more like a gift. If you're giving it to someone in the family, you might offer to make them some pancakes so they can try out your syrup!

What You'll Need

   2 pints unsweetened strawberries, fresh or frozen

   1 cup water

   1 tablespoon orange juice

   1/2 teaspoon cinnamon

   1 cup maple syrup

Note: You will need a 16-ounce bottle with a tightly fitting top. A clear bottle works best. Wash it very well either by hand or in the dishwasher.

What to do

   1. Puree strawberries, water, orange juice, and cinnamon in a blender, then add the maple syrup.

   2. Pour the mixture into a saucepan, and boil it over medium heat for about 5 minutes. Watch it closely so that the syrup doesn't burn.

   3. Remove from heat and pour the syrup into a clean glass bottle, using a funnel, and tightly screw on the top. Store until gift-giving time.

Bean and Seed Mosaic

It is amazing but true that beans and seeds are not just good for food. When they are put together in a design, they create a grand piece of artwork. Check out all the interesting beans and seeds at a local grocery store or organic food store. You will find beans with many shapes, sizes, textures, and colors. Collect an assortment of many kinds to make your mosaic unique!

What You'll Need

4 cups dry, unsalted beans and seeds

1 piece of cardboard or posterboard (about 10 inches by 10 inches)

White glue

What to do

1. Glue the beans and seeds to the cardboard or posterboard, creating your very own design. Make sure to cover all the cardboard.

2. Let it air-dry for about 3 hours.

Tip

You might want to cut the cardboard or posterboard into different sizes and shapes.

Pinecone Feeder

Makes about 6

This is a neat, simple bird feeder that will attract all kinds of birds. It is best to make and hang a feeder in the fall, when birds are hungry for yummy seeds. Hang it outside the kitchen window so the whole family can watch the feathered beauties. This also makes a great project to make with your friends or classmates. The only trick is finding the pinecone.

What You'll Need

1 pinecone

1/4 cup peanut butter

1 cup birdseed

6 inches of strong string or ribbon

What to do

1. Attach the ribbon to the cone. (Just tie it around the top.)

2. Spread the peanut butter all over the pinecone, using a butter knife. Make sure you get it squished into the cone.

3. Sprinkle the birdseed on the peanut butter.

4. Hang it up outside in a place that the birds can easily reach.

Flocks of Famished Feathered Friends

Birds eat *all* day long. That's their job. Chickadees, goldfinches, and nuthatches are all seed-eating birds. After finding a seed, a chickadee flies to a branch, holds the seed with his or her feet, and pecks at it to open the shell and get at the meat inside. A nuthatch ("nut-hatch"), who likes to sit upside down on the trunk of a tree, pokes a sunflower seed into a small hole in the bark, then pecks at the seed until it opens. Watch the birds eat their seeds. What do some birds do that's different from other birds?

Window Noodle Art

Makes about 6

Noodles come in all shapes and sizes. We know some of them by their Italian names (macaroni, rigatoni, etc.) and some by English names that describe what they look like (bow ties, wagon wheels, etc). You can make beautiful window art just by gluing your noodles together. These make great birthday gifts or window decorations for your room.

What You'll Need

5 cups noodles (You can get many different kinds from the grocery store.)

3 toothpicks

White craft glue

2 feet of string

What to do

1. Using a toothpick to apply the glue, glue your noodles together any way you like.

2. Allow them to dry for at least 2 hours, and hang them with 4-inch strands of string.

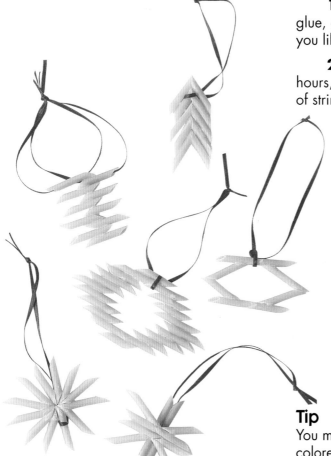

Call It Macaroni

In the late 13th century, German bakers made big, bulky shapes and figures out of noodle dough. These bakers went to Genoa, Italy, to sell their product, but the Italians claimed that the noodles were too big and too expensive. So the Germans made smaller noodles and sold them for a cheaper price. Ever since, people have been buying macaroni for many uses

Tip

You may want to hang your pasta art with colored ribbon instead of string.

Celebration Garlands

Makes 3

This is a perfect reason to throw a party! Gather up some neat dried fruits and nuts and a couple friends, and string together your very own celebration garlands. If you make them around Christmas, wrap them around your Christmas tree or give them as a present for someone special. They also make great wedding or graduation decorations.

What You'll Need

3 strings, each about 2 yards long

A heavy, strong needle

8 cups mixed dried fruits, nuts, and
    popped popcorn

What to do

1. Thread the needle with one piece of string, and tie a tight knot at the very end.

2. String the fruit, nuts, and popped popcorn in a nice pattern, putting different colors, shapes, and sizes next to each other.

3. Make two more garlands the same way.

Cinnamon Ornaments

Any kind of holiday or celebration calls for ornaments and decorations. You can make these for Christmas ornaments, birthday presents, or kitchen decorations. Try making a few with some friends, and see how much fun it can be!

What You'll Need

1/3 cup ground cinnamon

1/2 cup warm applesauce

What to do

1. Preheat the oven to 200°F.

2. Mix cinnamon and applesauce until mixture forms a ball. If the you need to, add more cinnamon.

3. Knead the dough on a cutting board sprinkled with cinnamon.

4. Roll out the dough to a 1/4-inch thickness, and cut out shapes with cookie cutters.

5. With a toothpick, make a hole in the top of each ornament for hanging.

6. Place the ornaments in the oven for about 3 hours, or air-dry them on a cooling rack for 6 days.

7. Decorate them with acrylic paint, glitter, etc. Thread a ribbon through each hole for hanging.

Pretzels

If you have ever been to New York City, you have probably seen all the pretzel stands on the sidewalks. Now you can make your own pretzels at home, using natural ingredients. It is a lot of fun to make funny shapes, like letters, numbers, people, or other interesting things. Just have fun with the dough and you will surely make great pretzels.

What You'll Need

1 envelope yeast

1/2 cup warm water

1 tablespoon molasses

1 teaspoon salt

1-1/2 cups whole wheat flour

1 egg, beaten

What to do

1. Preheat the oven to 425°F.

2. In a large mixing bowl, dissolve the yeast in the warm water. Add the molasses and salt, and mix well. Stir in the flour.

3. Knead the dough with clean hands to get all the air bubbles out. Roll thin, snake-like pieces of dough on a clean counter or table. Form shapes from the pieces, and place them on a baking sheet.

4. Brush a little of the beaten egg onto the shapes, and sprinkle them with coarse salt. Place them in the oven for about 10 minutes.

Santa's Cookies

Serves 1 St. Nicholas

Haven't you always wondered what kind of cookies Santa Claus really likes? We believe the jolly old fellow likes chocolate chip cookies. Now you can make something special for him...and set a couple aside for yourself, right?

What You'll Need

8 tablespoons (1 stick) sweet butter, softened

1/2 cup packed brown sugar

1/4 cup honey

1 egg

2 tablespoons orange juice

1/2 teaspoon vanilla extract

1-1/2 cups unbleached all-purpose flour

1/2 teaspoon baking soda

1/2 teaspoon salt

1/8 teaspoon ground cloves

1/2 teaspoon cinnamon

1 cup semisweet chocolate chips

What to do

1. Preheat the oven to 325°F.

2. Grease a cookie sheet, then cream the butter, sugar, and honey in a large mixing bowl. Get rid of as many lumps as you can!

3. Add the egg, orange juice, and vanilla to the butter mixture, and mix well.

4. Stir in the dry ingredients and keep stirring until the mixture is smooth. Fold in the chocolate chips.

5. Place spoonfuls of cookie batter on the cookie sheet. These cookies get bigger when they cook, so leave some space between them. Bake on the middle rack for about 10 to 12 minutes. Allow the cookies to cool a little bit before you remove them from the sheet, then place them on cooling racks. Makes about a dozen.

Orange-Clove Pomander

Makes 2

The winter holiday season is full of joy and memories. Make a couple of orange-clove pomanders to share with your friends or family. Pomanders smell great for a long time, and they make any room more festive.

What You'll Need

2 oranges

1-1/2 cups whole cloves

1 yard thin ribbon

What to do

1. Stick the cloves in the whole oranges, letting each clove have its own space. They look nicer when they are barely touching.

2. Let the pomanders sit for about a week, allowing the oranges to dry a little.

3. Make a loop of ribbon to hang each pomander by. Attach it (and a ribbon bow) to the top of the pomander with cloves.

Index of Recipes

Thanks, Kids

We'd like to thank the kids who cooked for the book—and let us take their pictures while they did.

Anna Bracken

Mary Bracken

Nathaniel Cannon

Katie Cummings

Eric Giesenschlag

Kevin Giesenschlag

Anna Jacobsen

Jeff Jacobsen

Ben Mackle

Tristan Mills

Megan Pearsall

Austin Sconyers-Snow

French Sconyers-Snow